The Life, Times, & Music™ Series

The Life, Times, & Music™ Series

Anna Hunt Graves

FRIEDMAN/FAIRFAX
PUBLISHERS

Acknowledgments

Thanks to my parents for their encouragement and to Marina Moskowitz for assisting me with my research

A FRIEDMAN GROUP BOOK

ISBN 1-56799-130-0

THE LIFE, TIMES, & MUSIC™ SERIES: FOLK
was prepared and produced by
Michael Friedman Publishing Group, Inc.
15 West 26th Street
New York, New York 10010

Editor: Benjamin Boyington
Art Director: Jeff Batzli
Designer: Andrea Karman
Photography Editor: Jennifer Crowe McMichael

Grateful acknowledgment is given to authors, publishers, and photographers for permission to reprint material. Every effort has been made to determine copyright owners of photographs and illustrations. In the case of any omissions, the publishers will be pleased to make suitable acknowledgments in future editions.

Printed in the United States of America

For bulk purchases and special sales, please contact:
Friedman/Fairfax Publishers
Attention: Sales Department
15 West 26th Street
New York, New York 10010
(212) 685-6610 FAX (212) 685-1307

CONTENTS

INTRODUCTION

"I guess all songs is folk songs—

I never heard no horse sing 'em."

—Country blues singer Bill Broonzy

Folk music is the music of the common people, and folk songs address social issues and concerns that affect ordinary individuals in their everyday lives. Songs in the folk genre tend to be musically simple and are usually played with acoustic instruments such as guitars, fiddles, banjos, mandolins, harmonicas, and dulcimers. Folk music

For many rural families, music often served as a pleasant diversion from work.

encompasses a variety of forms, including ballads, work songs, sea chanteys, cowboy songs, spirituals, calypso, blues, and folk-rock.

The history of folk music is directly tied to the lives of those who created and sang the songs, a diverse group of men and women who have made a vast contribution to American culture. The different styles that can be found within the folk genre reflect the ethnic and regional differences that existed within preindustrial

North America. Two primary influences came from British and Irish immigrants, who brought with them many folk songs of the British Isles, and African-Americans, who contributed spirituals and blues, among other forms of music. Many folk songs originated among working-class people in isolated rural areas where traditional tunes were passed down orally from one generation to another.

Community dances were a common form of entertainment in preindustrial North America.

Big Bill Broonzy made many folk blues recordings during the thirties and forties, but he did not achieve much recognition until the folk revival of the fifties. He died of cancer in 1958, just as he began to experience some success.

In the days before the advent of radio and the phonograph, people generally had to create their own entertainment. Music was often a part of community social gatherings such as barn raisings, dances, and religious revivals, and the occasional traveling show always featured musical entertainment. Men and women sometimes sang while they worked or as they relaxed around a fire. The traditional songs that emerged from rural North America during the early part of this century served as the foundation for the folk music that has been popularized over the past fifty years.

HILLBILLY MUSIC

According to American folklorist Archie Green, the term "hillbilly" began to be used in connection with music in the mid-1920s. While early country artists were generally labeled "hillbilly" performers, the category of hillbilly music included many traditional Southern folksingers as well. Country and folk have always been somewhat closely related, and the styles of numerous folk artists reflect both traditions. Hillbilly music became increasingly popular with the growth of the radio industry. During the mid-twenties, programs that featured live folksingers and musicians, such as Chicago's *National Barn Dance* and Nashville's *Grand Ole Opry*, captured the attention of radio audiences throughout the Midwest and the South.

During the summer of 1927, while touring the South seeking new performers, Ralph Peer (1892–1960), a talent scout for the Victor Talking Machine Company, came to Bristol, Tennessee, one of the few urban areas in the Appalachian Mountains. Peer spent about two weeks in Bristol recording a variety of individual performers and groups. These

sessions marked an important turning point in folk music, for among the unknown artists Peer discovered were the Carter Family and Jimmie Rodgers (1897–1933).

A.P. Carter (1891–1960), his wife, Sara (1898–1979), and his sister-in-law, Maybelle (1909–1978), who later married A.P.'s brother, came to Bristol from the hills of Virginia, where they had been performing at parties, church socials, and other local events for years. Sara usually led the singing while playing the autoharp or guitar, Maybelle harmonized with her and played lead guitar, and A.P. provided a bass or baritone vocal accompaniment. Within a few years of their recording debut, they were known nationwide for such compositions as "Wildwood Flower" (1928), "Will the Circle Be Unbroken" (1935), and "Keep on the Sunny Side" (1928). The melodies of their songs, along with Maybelle's innovative guitar work, served as inspiration for many future songwriters. Woody Guthrie, who often

Shows such as the *Grand Ole Opry,* which began in 1925 and can still be heard weekly to this day, attracted large studio audiences as well as countless radio listeners.

Often referred to as the "Father of Country Music," Jimmie Rodgers, shown here in his "Singing Brakeman" garb, composed and recorded more than a hundred songs. One of his most popular tunes was "T for Texas," also known as "Blue Yodel."

borrowed from other composers, used one of their tunes when he wrote the classic "This Land Is Your Land" (1940). During the 1930s, the Carters recorded for several record companies, including RCA Victor and Decca, and appeared on the powerful Mexican border radio stations that could be heard across the Southwest. When they stopped making records in 1941, the Carters had recorded more than three hundred songs together, creating a musical legacy that remains widespread today.

Jimmie Rodgers was the first hillbilly singer to become a national star. He was also one of RCA Victor's bestselling performers in the 1920s. Although his reign in the spotlight was relatively brief—he died of tuberculosis in 1933—the music he recorded had a tremendous impact on listeners across the country. Known as the "Singing Brakeman" because of his years as a railroad man, Rodgers was the first person to be elected to the Country Music Hall of Fame when it was established in 1961. The songs he recorded drew from a variety of sources, combining popular vaudeville material with traditional music and the blues songs Rodgers had learned from African-American field hands while he was growing up in rural Mississippi. His guitar techniques and distinctive yodeling style of singing attracted countless fans and influenced many future country and folk artists. Rodgers' amazing commercial success forced the music industry to recognize the existence of a vast market for traditional music.

THE FOLK SONG COLLECTORS

Many of the songs sung by the Carter Family were tunes derived from traditional sources, which the Carters arranged and copyrighted as their own compositions. After the group had become established as performers, A.P. Carter made a number of song-hunting trips, seeking out folk material that could be added to the Carter Family repertoire. By performing and recording these traditional songs, the Carters helped to preserve music that might otherwise have disappeared. While A.P. collected folk songs and tales in part for posterity, his primary motivation for doing so was to build up a large body of songs that the Carter Family could perform and record. Other men and woman took up the task of documenting folk material solely for the purpose of historical preservation.

Although folk music had been a part of rural American culture for hundreds of years, scholars and musicologists made few efforts to catalog folk songs until the late nineteenth century. In 1898, the American Folk Song Society was created for the purpose of preserving folk music, an art form that many believed was on the verge of extinction. This fear was soon proved to be false, however, for between 1910 and 1940, numerous folklorists gathered thousands of songs, many of which had never been written down, from different parts of the United States. These song hunters encountered such songs as "Barbara Allen," which first appeared in Scotland in the early 1600s, and "On Top of Old Smoky," another tune of Scottish origin dating back to 1788, which became a hit for the folk group the Weavers in 1951.

One influential song collector was an English folklorist named Cecil Sharp (1859–1924) who spent nearly a year gathering material in the Appalachian Mountains between 1916 and 1918. With the assistance of Maud Karpeles (1885–1976), Sharp obtained approximately sixteen hundred songs, many of which were included in his *English Folk Songs of the Southern Appalachians,* first published in 1917 (a larger, posthumous version, edited by Karpeles, appeared in 1932). In 1927, the poet Carl Sandburg (1878–1967), who often ended his poetry recitations by performing folk

Known primarily for his populist poetry, Carl Sandburg also performed and recorded traditional folk songs. He began collecting folk material while wandering around the United States during his youth.

songs, produced *The American Songbag*, one of the first collections of folk songs aimed at the public as opposed to a scholarly audience, drawing from his own collecting efforts as well as those of others.

One of the collectors who impressed Sandburg with his knowledge of cowboy songs was John Lomax, a scholar and ballad hunter who played a vital role in the history of folk music. Lomax dedicated a large part of his life to the preservation and promotion of American folk songs, collecting thousands of recordings for the Archive of American Folk Song, a collection of recordings and historical material related to folk music that had been established by the Library of Congress in 1928, and producing several published collections of folk material. His book *Cowboy Songs and Other Frontier Ballads*, which documented some of the songs of his adopted home state of Texas and sparked interest in regional folk culture, appeared in 1910 with an endorsement from former president Theodore Roosevelt. This anthology was the first collection of American folk music that included musical transcriptions as well as the lyrics of the songs. A second volume, entitled *Songs of the Cattle Trail and Cow Camp*, appeared in 1917, and in later years Lomax collaborated with his son Alan to produce *American Ballads and Folk Songs* (1934), *Negro Folk Songs as Sung by Leadbelly* (1935), *Our Singing Country* (1939), and *Folk Song, U.S.A.* (1947). Among the well-known songs that Lomax collected were "Home on the Range," "The Streets of Laredo," "Sweet Betsy from Pike," and "The Ballad of Jesse James."

JOHN LOMAX (1867–1948)

John Avery Lomax was born in Mississippi and moved with his family to Bosque County, Texas, when he was two years old. Lomax was entranced by the cowboy songs of Texas and began writing them down at an early age. While attending the University of Texas, he showed some of the songs he had collected to a professor, who dismissed them as "tawdry, cheap, and unworthy." He received no encouragement in his efforts to collect and preserve such music until 1906, when a teacher at Harvard took an interest in his efforts and introduced him to George Lyman Kittredge, one of the nation's foremost scholars in the study of Anglo-American folk songs. After completing his master's degree at Harvard, Lomax received a series of fellowships that enabled him to embark upon his mission of collecting folk songs of the West. In 1909, he appeared before the Modern Language Association to read an article entitled "Cowboy Songs of the Mexican Border," which was perhaps the first academic presentation of folk songs. The following year, Lomax published *Cowboy Songs and Other Frontier Ballads,* the first of several folk song collections he would produce over the next three decades.

In his narrative history of folk music, *The Incompleat Folksinger,* Pete Seeger tells the story of the time John Lomax attended a cattlemen's convention in the hopes of learning some of their songs. According to Seeger, one of the men got up and announced, "There's a man named Lomax here who wants to know if anyone knows some of the old cowboy songs. Why, everybody knows those damn fool songs, and only a bigger damn fool would try to collect them. I vote we adjourn to the bar." This anecdote illustrates only one of the many difficulties Lomax encountered in his efforts to preserve folk material, which for Lomax was a continuing and lifelong process. Although Lomax died in 1948, many of the songs he collected and recorded will live on forever, thanks to his dedication and perseverance.

In the early thirties, the only way to obtain recordings of folk songs was to find folksingers and record their performances. John Lomax installed this recording apparatus, provided by the Library of Congress, in the back of his car and used it to make a great number of field recordings.

Lomax spent a number of years traveling around the United States making field recordings that were later transcribed and compiled into book form. In the early thirties, his teenage son, Alan (1915–), joined him in his efforts, and the two set out to collect African-American folk songs from the South with a 350-pound (159kg) recording machine built into the back of their car. While visiting a Louisiana penitentiary, they met a black convict known as Leadbelly. The Lomaxes brought Leadbelly to New York, where he became one of the first African-American folk musicians to achieve national prominence. Leadbelly never achieved great commercial success, but he was a highly respected figure in the New York folk scene and was responsible for introducing such classic songs as "Goodnight Irene," "Midnight Special," and "Rock Island Line."

In 1934, John Lomax became the curator for the Archive of American Folk Song (sometimes referred to simply as the Archive of Folk Song). Together, John and Alan Lomax, who served as an assistant archivist after 1937, eventually contributed more than ten thousand songs collected during their years of fieldwork. While the music industry was suffering as a result of the Great Depression, national interest in traditional folk music and folk culture in general was on the rise. During the late 1930s, the Works Progress Administration (WPA),

LEADBELLY (1888–1949)

Huddie Ledbetter and Martha Promise were married in January 1935.

The spirit and power of Leadbelly are perhaps best expressed by Woody Guthrie: "The best and loudest singer I ever run onto his name was Huddie Ledbetter and we all called him Leadbelly, his arms was like big stove pipes, and his face was powerful and he picked the twelve-string guitar." Born in Mooringsport, Louisiana, Huddie Ledbetter, or Leadbelly, as he was more commonly known, became an extremely influential folksinger after being "discovered" by John and Alan Lomax while in prison in 1933. Leadbelly had grown up surrounded by poverty and racism, and had left home at the age of sixteen. As a child he had learned to play the accordion and the guitar, and while roaming the country as a young man he was exposed to jazz, blues, and traditional folk music. In 1918, he was convicted of assault and sent to a Texas prison where he remained for six years, until he was released after performing for the governor. In 1930, he was imprisoned again in Louisiana, where he remained until the Lomaxes arranged for him to be pardoned in 1934. That same year he embarked on a tour of Northern colleges with the Lomaxes, who used his blues-based performances as an example of African-American folk music. Some audiences had difficulty understanding his thick Southern accent, and occasionally his lyrics had to be "translated."

Although they helped Leadbelly to establish himself as a folksinger and songwriter, their relationship with him was somewhat paternalistic. They used him as their chauffeur on some of their song-collecting journeys, and later briefly employed him and his wife, Martha, as domestic servants. Leadbelly eventually settled in New York, where he became an important influence on other folk artists, among them Pete Seeger and Woody Guthrie. While he wrote or adapted numerous songs that went on to become folk standards, such as "Goodnight Irene," he also composed lesser-known songs of protest, many of them focusing on racism. One such song, "Bourgeois Blues," was written in the late thirties after he and some white friends were unable to find a hotel in Washington, D.C., that would accommodate an interracial group. In 1949, Leadbelly became ill while performing in Europe, and returned to New York. In December, he died of amyotrophic lateral sclerosis, also known as Lou Gehrig's disease, at the age of sixty-three, only months before the Weavers' version of "Goodnight Irene" became a million-seller.

BURL IVES (1909–)

Although they were colleagues in the folk music industry, Burl Ives (left) and Woody Guthrie were never friends.

Although Burl Ives began his career in entertainment as an actor, Americans in the 1940s knew him as a folksinger who popularized such songs as "The Erie Canal" and "Big Rock Candy Mountain." Born in Jasper County, Illinois, on June 14, 1909, Ives learned folk ballads from his grandmother while he was still a child. While in high school, he learned to play the banjo and he performed at school and local events. Ives was also a proficient football player, however, and when he entered an Illinois college in 1927, his goal was to become a football coach. After two years at school, he dropped out to travel around North America and Mexico, hitchhiking and hopping trains. During this odyssey, he learned to play the guitar and acquired a great deal of folk song material. After returning to school in Indiana for a brief period, Ives moved to New York, where he began studying theater and taking voice lessons at New York University.

In the summer of 1938 Ives was "discovered" by a producer who helped him get his first Broadway role. He went on to act in other shows while simultaneously pursuing a career as a folksinger. While living in New York, Ives became acquainted with some of the local folk artists, including Woody Guthrie, Pete Seeger and Lee Hays. In 1940, he was given his own radio show on CBS, which was named *The Wayfarin' Stranger* after one of his songs. This program was extremely popular, and it lasted for two years, until Ives joined the army to serve as an entertainer. After World War II ended, Ives continued his acting as well as his folksinging. By the time he published his autobiography, *The Wayfarin' Stranger,* in 1948, he had become a nationally known entertainer.

Although Burl Ives was at one time a part of the leftist element of New York's folk community, he incurred its wrath in 1950 when he willingly testified as an informant before the House Un-American Activities Committee (HUAC) during its investigation of the supposed connection between folk music and Communism. Because he chose to cooperate with the committee, Ives' appearance before HUAC had virtually no effect on his career as a performer; Pete Seeger and other artists who stood up to the investigators were not so fortunate. Ives made a number of films before returning to Broadway in 1954 to perform in *Show Boat.* The following year, he was praised for his stage performance as Big Daddy in *Cat on a Hot Tin Roof,* a role he later revived on film. In the late 1950s, Ives received an Academy Award for his performance in *The Big Country.* Although he reached his peak of popularity as a folksinger in the late 1940s, he continued making records into the 1960s.

one of the pioneer programs of Roosevelt's New Deal, funded a number of folk-related projects, including the Folklore Studies of the Federal Writers' Project; the Federal Music Project, directed by musicologist Charles Seeger (1886–1979), Pete Seeger's father; and the Archive of Folk Song.

In 1939, two years after Alan Lomax began his work at the Archive at the age of twenty-two, he started producing *Wellsprings of America,* a weekly syndicated show about folk music on CBS radio's *Columbia School of the Air.* Through this program, he reintroduced Americans to many traditional folk songs and exposed the public to such folk artists as Leadbelly, Pete Seeger, and Josh White (1915–1969). A few years before his radio show went on the air, Alan encouraged an actor named Burl Ives, who became a popular folksinger during the 1940s, to perform and record folk material. Lomax taught Ives some of his best-known songs, including "Blue Tail Fly." He also continued to make field recordings, documenting the great blues musicians Muddy Waters and Son House, among others. While Lomax helped a number of folk artists to achieve public recognition, his greatest discovery took place in 1940, the year he introduced listeners across the nation to the man commonly recognized as the greatest American folksinger of all: the legendary Woody Guthrie.

As a young boy, folk artist Josh White spent several years traveling throughout the South with various blind blues musicians and learning to play the guitar.

WOODY GUTHRIE (1912–1967)

I am out to sing songs that will prove to you that this is your world,... no matter what color, what size you are, how you are built.... And the songs I sing are made up for the most part by all sorts of folks just about like you.

—Woody Guthrie

Woodrow Wilson Guthrie was born on July 14, 1912, in Okemah, Oklahoma, and his early years were marked by tragedies. By the time he was fourteen, his older sister had perished in a fire, his mother had been institutionalized with the same disorder that would lead to his own death years later, and his father was experiencing serious financial difficulties. After a few years of being adopted by different families, Guthrie went on the road for the first time, traveling around the Southwest performing odd jobs. In 1933, he settled down long enough to marry and father two children, but by the mid-thirties, when the Depression was at its peak, he grew restless and left his family to head west.

Guthrie traveled to California, where he lived with relatives and frequented migrant worker camps resembling those described in John Steinbeck's famous novel *The Grapes of Wrath*. Woody's uncle Jeff Guthrie had taught him how to play the guitar as a teenager, and

The music of Woody Guthrie's songs tended to be quite simple, allowing listeners to focus more closely on the meaning of his lyrics.

within several years of picking up the instrument Woody was writing his own songs. Between the mid-thirties and the mid-fifties, he composed more than a thousand songs. He derived his style of playing, as well as the melodies for some of his compositions, from the Carter Family. In Los Angeles he managed to get a job appearing on the radio with his cousin Jack Guthrie, who later had a hit with one of Woody's songs, "Oklahoma Hills." Soon Woody was the costar of a half-hour program on KFVD that allowed him to develop his easy-going style of performing, which mixed singing with rambling anecdotes that expressed his personal opinions, referred to by Guthrie as his "Cornpone Philosophy." This job also brought him together with Cisco Houston (1918–1961), a lifelong friend who went on to record and popularize many of Guthrie's compositions.

While working at KFVD, Woody was exposed to radical politics, and by the late thirties, he was playing regularly at union meetings and political rallies. He didn't seem to affiliate himself with any particular group, and he would sing for anybody who was willing to listen. On one occasion when he was asked to play at a Communist party meeting, after being told

Woody Guthrie did not seem like a family man—he was well known for his habit of taking to the road with little or no notice. Nevertheless, he was married three times and had children from each marriage.

that it was going to be a left-wing event, he replied, "Left-wing, right-wing, chicken wing—it's all the same to me." In addition to performing for radical gatherings, Guthrie wrote a column called "Woody Sez," in the style of humorist Will Rogers, for *People's World*, a daily Communist newspaper. Through his connections with the left, Woody met Will Geer (1902–1978), an actor and political activist who was fond of folk music. Toward the end of the decade, with Geer's encouragement, Woody moved to New York, where his career as a folksinger finally began to take shape.

In New York, on March 3, 1940, Will Geer organized a "Grapes of Wrath" benefit for California migrant workers. The show, which featured such artists as Burl Ives, Josh White, Aunt Molly Jackson (an Appalachian coal miner's wife who wrote labor songs), Leadbelly, and Woody Guthrie, was a significant event in the history of folk music, not because of the particular performances, but because of the individuals whose paths crossed on that particular evening. That night marked Pete Seeger's first concert appearance and

his first opportunity to see (and hear) Woody Guthrie perform, which was an inspiring moment for Seeger. Alan Lomax would later describe the meeting of these two folksingers as "the renaissance of American folk song." Lomax, who was quite impressed by Guthrie's performance, was also introduced to him after the show. While Guthrie and Seeger would go on to become musical collaborators, Lomax would soon be responsible for changing the course of Guthrie's career.

Alan Lomax loved Woody's music, as well as the hillbilly persona Guthrie projected. He invited Woody to appear on his nationally syndicated radio show, and recorded hours of Woody talking and singing for the Archive of Folk Song. Although these sessions would not be made available to the public until the mid-1960s, Lomax convinced a producer from RCA Victor to record Guthrie,

Folksingers like Woody Guthrie often performed topical protest songs at labor union rallies such as this one, which took place in Illinois in 1932.

Although Guthrie's formal education was incomplete, he was an avid reader, and despite his hillbilly demeanor and persona, he was extremely knowledgeable about politics and social issues.

In this scene from the Woody Guthrie film biography *Bound for Glory* (based on his autobiography), Woody and a friend entertain a group of children on the side of a road.

which resulted in the production of a collection entitled *Dust Bowl Ballads*. Released as a set of twelve 78-rpm records, *Dust Bowl Ballads* sold relatively few copies; nevertheless it represents the first serious attempt to record social protest material, featuring songs such as "Do Re Mi," "Dust Bowl Refugee," and "I Ain't Got No Home" that addressed the problems faced by migrant laborers during the Depression. Around the same time, Guthrie and Pete Seeger collaborated with Lomax on a book of protest songs called *Hard Hitting Songs for Hard Hit People*. Lomax, however, was unable to find anyone willing to publish the work because of its overtly political content, and it did not appear in print until 1962. With encouragement from his second wife and from Lomax, Guthrie wrote his own book, a colorful autobiography entitled *Bound for Glory*, published in 1943 and made into a movie in 1976.

Woody continued to compose songs throughout the forties, and a great deal of his work from that era contained political and social commentary. When World War II began in Europe, Woody adopted a pacifist stance and became part of a group known as the Almanac Singers, who performed peace songs that were often critical of President Roosevelt. The group's opposition to the war echoed the sentiments of such left-wing organizations as the American Communist Party, whose members initially felt that the United

MOE ASCH (1905–1986) AND FOLKWAYS RECORDS

Born in Poland, Moses "Moe" Asch discovered John Lomax's *Cowboy Songs and Other Frontier Ballads* while he was a student in Europe during the early twenties and developed a strong interest in folk music. Sometime after 1925, Asch came to the United States, where he manufactured recording equipment in New York. Many years later, in 1939, he was able to start his own independent record label, Asch Records, which featured various folk and ethnic performers, including Burl Ives. When the label went bankrupt, he and a partner created Disc Records, offering a slightly wider variety of music. Unfortunately for Asch, this company also succumbed to debt. After declaring bankruptcy a second time, Asch founded a third label, Folkways Records, in 1947. The central tenet behind Folkways was, as Asch put it, "folk music as a manifestation of American culture. ...[Folkways Records] listens, and if it finds that the person has something legitimate to say, it is published." Folkways produced hundreds of songs by Leadbelly and Woody Guthrie, and at least sixty-three albums by Pete Seeger alone. By keeping production costs low and prices slightly higher than normal, Asch was able to produce an astounding number of records, recording not only folk music, but also jazz, poetry, language lessons, and many other kinds of material. He died in 1986, with the Folkways catalog comprising more than twenty-five hundred recordings, an average of more than a record a week for almost forty years. Currently, the label's catalog is owned by the Smithsonian Institution, and many of the original folk albums Asch helped make possible are now available on compact disc.

States should not become involved in the conflict. After Nazi Germany invaded Russia and the Japanese attacked Pearl Harbor in 1941, most leftists began to support the war effort. The Almanac Singers switched to patriotic material, with Guthrie pasting a sign on his guitar that read *THIS MACHINE KILLS FASCISTS.* During the war, Woody met his second wife, Marjorie Mazia (1917–), with whom he had a son, Arlo (1947–), and he served as a Merchant Marine alongside his close friend Cisco Houston. It was at this time that Guthrie began recording for Moses Asch, founder of Folkways Records, making trips to the studio in between tours of duty at sea.

Guthrie went on to record approximately two hundred songs for Folkways, including his best-known composition, "This Land Is Your Land," which was originally written as a parody of Irving Berlin's "God Bless America." By the 1950s, Woody had become a legendary figure with a musical style and a personality that appealed to a wide range of people, forming a link between the rural and urban cultures of America. After growing up in Oklahoma, he spent many years in Los Angeles and New York; for most of his life he seemed unable to tolerate staying in any one place for very long before getting the urge to take to the road. Sadly, he was finally compelled to settle down when he was hospitalized in 1952 with a neurological disease known as Huntington's chorea. Over the next fifteen years his mind and body slowly deteriorated, and in October 1967, at the age of fifty-five, Woody Guthrie died.

PETE SEEGER (1919–)

One of Woody's cohorts from the early forties up until his death was Pete Seeger, a gangly New Englander whom many consider to be the father of modern folk music. While Guthrie played an important role as a transitional figure who helped bring attention to a more traditional and topical style of folksinging, Seeger's political awareness and his commitment to the use of music as a political weapon made him the champion of the social protest song. Like many other folk artists, Seeger was undoubtedly influenced by Guthrie—he paid Guthrie a direct tribute by placing a slogan on his banjo

Few performers can compete with Pete Seeger's enthusiasm and exuberance on stage.

that read *THIS MACHINE SURROUNDS HATE AND FORCES IT TO SURRENDER*. While Guthrie's greatest contribution to American folk music was his songwriting, Seeger became the driving force behind the urban folk revival as well as a visible performer and political activist.

Born in New York on May 3, 1919, Peter Seeger came from an aristocratic family that valued the fine arts, especially music. His father, Charles Seeger, was a well-known musicologist and his mother, Constance, was an accomplished violinist. Pete rebelled against his parents' classical background by learning to play the banjo while attending a private school in New England. During his high school years, Pete also developed an interest in journalism and radical politics, subscribing to *New Masses*, a Communist literary magazine. He entered Harvard in 1936, but within two years became bored with school and dropped out to pursue a career as a newspaperman. Unable to find a job, Seeger spent much of his time practicing the banjo.

Meanwhile, Charles Seeger had divorced his first wife to marry Ruth Crawford (1901–1953), a composer and piano teacher. In the mid-thirties, they moved to Washington, D.C., where they were among the many intellectuals who "discovered" folk music. The Seegers became acquainted with Alan Lomax, and Ruth helped transcribe many of his field recordings for publication. While on business in New York, Lomax introduced Pete to a small community of folk artists that included Leadbelly and Aunt Molly Jackson. In 1939, Lomax offered Seeger a job assisting him at the Archive of Folk Song, where he was exposed to an even greater variety of folk music. The following year, Pete met Woody Guthrie at the Grapes of Wrath benefit, and the two took off on a cross-country trip to "discover" the United States.

When Seeger returned to New York in late 1940, he met Lee Hays (1914–1981), a former teacher and song leader (he led the student body in singing songs at school meetings) from the radical Commonwealth Labor College in Arkansas. Seeger's singing and musicianship had improved greatly during his travels, and he and Hays decided to form a group that became known as the Almanac Singers. Hays suggested the name, pointing out that most rural families owned a Bible and an almanac—one to serve as a guide to the next world, the other to this one. Although the group originally consisted of Seeger, Hays, Millard Lampell, and Peter Hawes, it later included Woody Guthrie, Cisco Houston, Bess

HOOTENANNY

The word "hootenanny" first appeared in the 1947 *Webster's New World Dictionary of the American Language*, where it was defined simply as "a gathering of folk singers." Several years earlier, a Democratic group in Seattle used the term to describe their political fund-raising events, which offered various activities and forms of entertainment. The first of these gatherings, held during the summer of 1940, was advertised in a local paper as follows:

The New Dealer's
Midsummer Hootenanny
You Might Even Be Surprised
Dancing Refreshment Door Prizes
Uncertainty

While touring the West Coast as the Almanac Singers in 1941, Pete Seeger and Woody Guthrie performed at one of these fund-raisers. When they returned to New York, they adopted the term "hootenanny" for the rent parties they held regularly to raise money to support themselves. When the organization People's Songs, Inc. was formed by Seeger following World War II, hootenannies were staged to help with its expenses, as well as to benefit folk publications like *Sing Out!* The postwar hootenannies soon became extremely popular, and the performers were forced to seek larger venues in order to accommodate their audiences. One of the first large-scale "hoots," as they were sometimes called, was held in 1947 at Irving Plaza in New York and featured performances by Seeger, Guthrie, Sonny Terry, Brownie McGhee, Alan Lomax, Bess Lomax Hawes, and other artists.

The term "hootenanny" was further popularized during the 1950s as hootenannies began to be held on college campuses across America. Coffeehouses that emerged in urban areas also provided a setting for these events. In New York during the early sixties, a folk club called the Bitter End (which is still in operation today) helped to keep the tradition alive by holding weekly hootenannies featuring performances by professional and amateur folksingers. In 1963, ABC purchased the rights to this concept, as well as the name, from the owners of the club to create the *Hootenanny* television show, sponsored by Procter & Gamble. The half-hour show was taped at a different college each week and featured three or four artists who were occasionally accompanied by the college students that made up the audience.

This concept disgusted some folksingers, such as Pete Seeger, who described *Hootenanny* as "a gay variety show where nothing controversial would ever be presented." His description was somewhat accurate, for the show initially turned down an interracial folk group called the Tarriers, until the show's producers were pressured into letting them perform. Seeger himself was never invited to appear on the program because he had been blacklisted during the McCarthy era. Other popular folk artists, including Joan Baez, Peter, Paul and Mary, the Kingston Trio, and Bob Dylan, supported him by boycotting the show. The show was popular for a short time, but its appeal quickly faded and it was canceled in 1964.

In addition to his musical accomplishments, Pete Seeger is the author of several books, including *American Favorite Ballads, How to Play the Five-String Banjo,* and *The Incompleat Folksinger.*

Lomax Hawes (1921–) (Alan's sister), Josh White, Agnes "Sis" Cunningham (1909–), Sonny Terry (1911–1986), and Brownie McGhee (1915–). Membership in the Almanac Singers fluctuated wildly, and for a while Seeger and Guthrie toured alone under that name.

Many of those who belonged to the Almanacs lived communally in a Greenwich Village loft known as Almanac House, where they created songs that were specifically designed to garner support for leftist social and political goals. During World War II, the Almanacs began holding Sunday afternoon concerts, which they called "hootenannies," in the basement of their home. As the first urban folk group, the Almanac Singers helped to initiate the urban folk revival that flourished during the 1950s.

In early 1941, they recorded their first album, *Songs for John Doe,* a collection of antiwar songs. A large part of the Almanac Singers' repertoire also consisted of labor songs, which they performed at rallies and union meetings across the country. Soon after their first record appeared, they recorded *Talking Union*, an album of songs that featured class-conscious lyrics set to traditional folk tunes.

As the Soviet Union and the United States were drawn into World War II, the politics of the Almanac Singers shifted, along with those of many liberals whose pacifist leanings were outweighed by their desire to destroy fascism. The Almanacs' first record was withdrawn from the market, and in 1942 an album called *Dear Mr. President*, which expressed full support for the war effort, was released. After the group switched from pacifist songs to patriotic songs, its popularity began to increase. The group performed on network radio and Office of War Information programs and were offered a recording contract from Decca Records. The success of the Almanacs was undermined when the media began to attack them for their peace songs and their connections with the Communist Party. Suddenly they were shunned by the music industry, and the group dissolved as most of its members joined branches of the armed forces. Their last two albums, *Sod Buster Ballads* and *Deep Sea Chanteys*, consisted of noncontroversial traditional material.

Pete Seeger was drafted into the Army in mid-1942, and spent most of his time serving with USO entertainers in the South Pacific. During this time he also married a Japanese-American named Toshi Ohta, who gave birth to their first child in 1944. Soon after returning home, Seeger founded an organization called People's Songs, Inc., a songwriters' union of sorts that was designed to offer an alternative to the existing popular entertainment monopoly. In 1946, Seeger, Hays, and others began producing *The People's Songs Bulletin* as a means of promoting and spreading traditional folk songs as well as more contemporary songs of social and political protest. Based in New York, People's Songs, Inc. had chapters in other cities, including Chicago and Los Angeles. The organization and the *Bulletin* ran out of money in 1949 after lending support to the unsuccessful presidential campaign of Progressive party candidate Henry Wallace. Despite its failure, People's Songs was able to attract several thousand members at its peak, and it represents an admirable attempt to counter the status quo of the music industry.

Although Pete Seeger also plays other instruments, including the guitar and the recorder, the banjo has always been his favorite. He discovered the four-string tenor banjo in high school, and was later introduced to the five-string banjo by the painter Thomas Hart Benton.

Although circulation of the *Bulletin* never broke two thousand, the publication served as the forerunner for a folk song magazine called *Sing Out!*, which was first published in 1950 and still exists today.

While working with People's Songs, Pete Seeger and Lee Hays began rehearsing with Fred Hellerman (1927–) and Ronnie Gilbert (1926–), two young performers who were relative newcomers to the New York folk scene. Hellerman and Gilbert, who knew each other from attending a left-wing summer camp called Wo-Chi-Ca (Workers' Children's Camp), were both in their early twenties. The four artists performed in public together for the first time in 1948, calling themselves the No-Name Quartet. The group's trademark sound was already apparent—the combination of Gilbert's alto, Seeger's tenor, Hellerman's baritone, and Hays' bass harmonized perfectly, while Seeger and Hellerman provided instrumental accompaniment on banjo and guitar. The following year, they adopted the name "the Weavers," which was the title of a German play about a strike led by nineteenth-century textile workers. In December 1949, they were offered a job at the Village Vanguard, with a starting salary of two hundred dollars a week plus all the free hamburgers they could eat. Leadbelly had just died, and they chose to honor him by ending each show with a rendition of his song "Goodnight Irene."

The Weavers' performances at the Vanguard were not immediately successful, but after Alan Lomax brought Carl Sandburg to one of their shows, the group began to achieve public recognition. The press quoted Sandburg's ringing endorsement: "The Weavers are out of the grass roots of America. I salute them for their great work in authentic renditions of...folk songs.... When I hear America singing, the Weavers are there." The Weavers were signed to Decca Records, and soon they were stars with a national following. Their early hits included Woody Guthrie's "So Long, It's Been Good to Know You" (1951); "Goodnight Irene" (1950), which was recorded by the pop star Frank Sinatra shortly after the Weavers' version became popular; the South African chant "Wimoweh" (1951); and "On Top of Old Smoky" (1951). In the liner notes for one of their albums there is the comment, "Folk singing is not new at all, for it has been going on since there were folks on earth to sing"; yet for the many Americans who were unfamiliar with folk music, these songs were new and refreshing. During a short period of time in the early 1950s, the Weavers sold millions of records and

Pete Seeger at an anti–Vietnam War rally in New York's Times Square in 1969. Calling himself a "cultural guerilla," Seeger has associated himself with numerous political causes throughout his career.

Unlike their predecessors the Almanac Singers, the Weavers spent many hours in rehearsal so that they could deliver polished musical arrangements, which they performed at nightclubs in Hollywood, Las Vegas, and New York.

appeared on numerous radio and television shows, including *The Milton Berle Show,* which was one of America's most popular programs. They also continued making public performances in nightclubs all over the country, unaware that their success would soon quickly evaporate due to the political atmosphere of the 1950s, specifically the rise of Senator Joseph McCarthy, and the leftist leanings and associations not only of the Weavers but of the folk movement as a whole.

FOLK MUSIC AND THE LEFT

The concept of using music as a political tool is by no means new. In the eighteenth century, the English political writer Andrew Fletcher remarked, "Give me the making of the songs of a nation, and I care not who makes its laws." This idea that music can be used to convey socially significant messages (and perhaps even change or control the political current) has become a firmly established tradition in

Like Pete Seeger, Joan Baez is not only a performer, but a political activist. Her song "Joe Hill" celebrates the life and work of a songwriter for the labor union Industrial Workers of the World.

American folk music. At the Woodstock Music Festival in 1969, Joan Baez sang a song called "Joe Hill," which told the story of a songwriter for the Industrial Workers of the World (IWW), commonly known as the Wobblies. Established in 1905, the Wobblies were a radical coalition of laborers with a membership that grew to 150,000 prior to World War I. In 1909, they began distribution of what was known as the *Little Red Song Book*, formally titled *I.W.W. Songs: Songs of the Workers to Fan the Flames of Discontent.* The Wobblies often sang in public to counteract the Salvation Army bands that often tried to overpower IWW speakers with their music. Many of Joe Hill's songs were parodies of Salvation Army hymns with blatantly political lyrics, featuring titles such as "Nearer My Job to Thee." Shortly before he was executed in 1915 for a murder he may or may not have committed, Joe Hill sent a message to the president of the IWW, saying, "Don't waste time in mourning—organize!" The spirit of his radical compositions and political activism became a source of inspiration for folk artists like Woody Guthrie and Pete Seeger.

Another folk artist who combined traditional material with political sentiments was Aunt Molly Jackson (1880–1960), a union organizer and songwriter from the coal mining country of rural eastern Kentucky who moved to New York in the early 1930s, after her activism made her unpopular with local authorities. Alan Lomax claimed that Jackson's protest songs were comparable to those of Woody Guthrie, noting that her compositions were often "more passionate" and tended to "cut deeper." Responsible for such labor songs as "Poor Miner's Farewell," "Hungry Disgusted Blues," and "I Am a Union Woman," Jackson was sought out by numerous folk song collectors during the later years of her life. Although she never profited from her musical endeavors, several hundred of her songs were recorded by the Lomaxes for the Archive of American Folk Song. Poor and relatively unknown, Jackson died at the age of eighty in 1960, just as the folk music revival was gathering momentum.

While Jackson was unable to take advantage of the increasing national interest in traditional music, her younger half-sister Sarah Ogan Gunning (1910–), who also came from the mountains of Kentucky, became a prominent folk figure in the mid-1960s. Like Jackson, Gunning wrote about the suffering of the coal miners and their efforts to unionize. During the thirties, she became known for such songs as "I Am a Girl of Constant Sorrow," "Down on the Picket Line," and "I Hate the Capitalist System." Gunning's brother Jim Garland, a miner and labor organizer, also composed protest songs that drew from the folk tradition, including "I Don't Want Your Millions, Mister" (written in 1932). Another enduring labor anthem of the Depression, "Which Side Are You On," was written by Florence Reece (1900–1986) after a violent miner's strike that failed in 1931 and was later adapted for use by civil rights activists. Songs such as these evoked a new spirit of resistance that was beginning to emerge. Folk songwriters like Jackson and Gunning understood that music could be used to educate as well as to entertain an audience.

Urban intellectuals were also beginning to recognize the capability of music to convey a message and raise the consciousness of the masses. During the thirties, Charles Seeger and some of his radical colleagues established the

Composers' Collective, which published the *Workers' Songbook,* in which it was proclaimed, "Music is a weapon in the class struggle." While members of the Collective generally disliked folk music, preferring highbrow protest songs based on classical forms, the group created a legacy for left-wing musical organizations such as the Almanac Singers and People's Songs. The Collective was also closely linked to the American Communist Party, and when the former organization folded in 1936, many of its Communist affiliates turned to folk music as a means of inspiration and a vehicle for voicing their beliefs.

In 1933, a left-wing journalist named Michael Gold complained of the Communist Party's need for proletarian songwriters like Joe Hill. Less than a decade later, the Almanac Singers, the first well-known folk artists to be associated with the Communist movement, appeared on the scene. When asked if he was a Communist, Woody Guthrie used to say, "That ain't necessarily so, but it is true that I've been in the red all my life." Whether the individuals who made up the Almanacs actually belonged to the Communist Party was more or less irrelevant—they were heavily influenced by the party's ideas, and their music generally expressed and reaffirmed its radical political outlook. As this relationship

between folk music and Communism became more apparent, the government began to pay more attention to the careers of certain performers, particularly Pete Seeger.

Under the instruction of J. Edgar Hoover, the FBI kept tabs on Seeger throughout World War II, and in the late forties it scrutinized People's Songs, which it suspected was a Communist front. In one report on the organization it was noted that "they play folk songs... where the hoity-toity red intellectuals gather." The House Un-American Activities Committee (HUAC) also began to collect testimony linking People's Songs with Communism. Unknown to Seeger, some of the individuals involved with People's Songs became informants for the FBI. In 1949, a concert held in Peekskill, New York, featuring Paul Robeson, Seeger, and other folk artists, turned into a full-scale riot when angry locals attacked the performers because of their Communist connections. Robeson, an African-American actor and folksinger whose career had begun in the mid-1920s, was well known for his rendition of the song

The Industrial Workers of the World meet in New York's Union Square to express their sympathy for striking workers in Colorado. Meetings like this one often featured musical performances by union members as well as established folksingers.

"Ol' Man River" in the musical *Show Boat* and for his performance in a 1939 radio broadcast entitled *Ballad for Americans*. During the late forties, he played a leading role in the founding of the left-wing Progressive Party and was an ardent supporter of civil rights. Robeson was sharply criticized by conservatives for his political activities, and in 1950 his passport was revoked by HUAC (it was returned to him in 1958).

In the early 1950s, as the United States became involved in the Korean War, anti-Communist sentiment grew at an alarming rate. A telling anti-Communist joke from this period describes two party members planning a meeting; one says to the other, "You bring the Negro and I'll bring the folksinger." With its nationwide popularity, Seeger's new group, the Weavers, offered red-baiters a vulnerable target.

A 1949 concert held in Peekskill, New York, and featuring Paul Robeson, Pete Seeger, and other folksingers exploded in violence when anti-Communist locals and veterans converged on the scene to protest the leftist artists' performance.

THE WEAVERS—
VICTIMS OF McCARTHYISM

Although the majority of the Weavers' music was not overtly political, the members of the group were associated with radical causes, and they believed that music could be used to enact change. As Ronnie Gilbert put it, "We felt that if we sang loud enough and strong enough and hopefully enough, somehow it would make a difference." The release of the Weavers' first records in mid-1950 coincided with the appearance of *Red Channels: The Report of Communist Influence on Radio and Television*, which listed the names of more than a hundred writers and entertainers who were reportedly associated with the Communist movement. Alan Lomax, who had been working for Decca, moved to England for several years to avoid the Communist witch-hunts that ensued. Seeger was mentioned in *Red Channels*, along with Burl Ives and Josh White, both of whom later testified before HUAC and were consequently ostracized by the leftist folk community. The Weavers had been offered a weekly television series on NBC, but following the publication of *Red Channels*, the offer was with-

The original Weavers pose for a photo on the evening of their tremendously successful reunion concert at Carnegie Hall on Christmas Eve, 1955.

drawn. By the end of 1951, many of the Weavers' scheduled performances were canceled as a result of increasing controversy over their blacklisting. Early in the following year, Harvey Matusow, an informant who had previously been in charge of the People's Songs Music Center, appeared in front of HUAC and swore under oath that all four Weavers were either current or former members of the Communist Party. The Decca label would no longer record the group, and stopped producing the albums they had previously released, in spite of record sales that were in the millions. The Weavers disbanded at the end of 1952.

On Christmas Eve, 1955, the Weavers staged a successful comeback concert at Carnegie Hall. That same year, Pete Seeger was summoned before HUAC. He chose to invoke the First Amendment, which includes the

Harvey Matusow, seen here on a picket line supporting the International Longshoremen's Association, worked undercover for the FBI in many allegedly Communist organizations.

Following his conviction on multiple counts of contempt of Congress, Pete Seeger enters a New York courtroom with his banjo slung over his shoulder to hear his sentence.

freedom of speech, to defend himself and his refusal to answer the committee's questions. (Many people who were called before the committee chose to invoke the Fifth Amendment so as not to have to report on their friends and acquaintances. Seeger, however, was an exception—he chose to invoke the First Amendment in order to explain to the committee why he was not going to answer their questions.) Two years later he was indicted for contempt of Congress, and after reluctantly recording a jingle for a cigarette commercial with the Weavers, he left the group. The other Weavers continued to tour and record, with a succession of replacements for Seeger, until 1963. Seeger was later tried, found guilty, and sentenced to a prison term of a year and a day. Although his case was eventually dismissed on a technicality, he continued to suffer from the effects of being blacklisted. He did not appear on television until 1967, when he performed on *The Smothers Brothers' Comedy Hour*, and even then he was not allowed to sing his antiwar composition "Waist Deep in the Big Muddy." After leaving the Weavers, Seeger pursued a solo career, carrying on the tradition of social protest by involving himself in civil rights activities, anti–Vietnam War efforts, the antinuclear movement, and environmental concerns. Today Seeger continues to perform and lend his name to a variety of humanitarian causes.

THE URBAN FOLK REVIVAL

The origins of the urban folk revival can be traced back to the 1940s, when folk communities were beginning to take root in such cities as Boston, San Francisco, and especially New York, where the Almanac Singers held their weekly hootenannies, which attracted sizable crowds. By the mid-forties, amateur and professional folk artists were gathering on a regular basis to sing and play in New York's Washington Square Park. When the Weavers became a household name in the early fifties, interest in folk music spread rapidly across the country. In 1955, guitar sales in the United States reached half a million, and the first folk coffeehouse opened in Philadelphia. Over the next few years, the initial excitement of rock and roll started to wane—as Elvis joined the army; Jerry Lee Lewis scandalized the country by marrying his thirteen-year-old cousin; Buddy Holly, the Big Bopper, and Richie Valens died in a plane crash; and payola scandals rocked the industry—and many young people turned to other forms of musical entertainment.

In 1956 a young folksinger named Harry Belafonte set off a calypso craze when he recorded a string of hits that included "Day-O (The Banana Boat Song)" and "Jamaica Farewell." Belafonte was born in New York, but his parents were from the Caribbean, where he had spent part of his childhood. Capitol Records signed him as a pop vocalist when he was just out of college, but he was unsatisfied by popular music and left the label. Within a

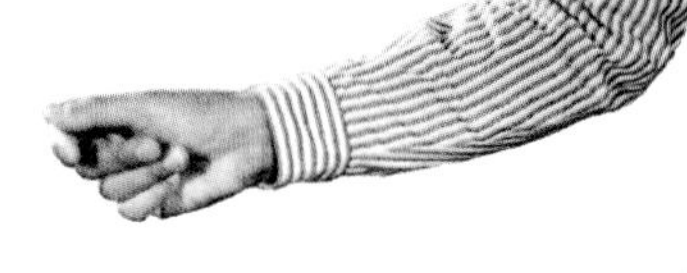

Entertainer Harry Belafonte, shown here rehearsing for his television special, made numerous appearances on programs such as *The Ed Sullivan Show* during the late fifties.

A group of young people gather in New York's Washington Square Park for an informal folk jamboree.

ELIZABETH COTTEN (1893–)

Elizabeth "Libba" Cotten taught herself to play the guitar as a child growing up in North Carolina. After marrying at the age of fifteen, she gave up music until the late 1940s, when she and her husband were divorced and she moved to Washington, D.C., to find work. Cotten was employed as a domestic servant by Charles and Ruth Seeger, whose children Mike and Peggy overheard her playing "Freight Train," a song she had written when she was twelve years old. The Seegers encouraged her to perform and record her material, and she went on to become known for her songwriting as well as her distinctive style of guitar playing. In addition to playing her guitar upside down (she was left-handed, but she played instruments strung for right-handed musicians), Cotten created her own methods of two- and three-finger picking that have influenced many folk and blues guitarists.

few years, he developed a repertoire of American and West Indian folk songs that resulted in a series of records released by RCA Victor. Belafonte's album *Calypso* sold a million copies, spawning a number of imitators and establishing him as an important folk artist.

Other performers who were less popular but nonetheless influential in terms of the folk revival were Odetta and Elizabeth Cotten, two African-American folksingers who accompanied themselves on the guitar. Admired by artists such as Pete Seeger and Harry Belafonte, Odetta first attracted the public's attention during the early fifties when she played at clubs in San Francisco, New York, and Los Angeles. Her first album, *Odetta Sings Ballads and Blues*, appeared in 1956 and was followed by several television appearances and a successful tour of the United States and Canada. Elizabeth "Libba" Cotten, who was well into her fifties when she began performing, also inspired artists interested in traditional American music with her 1957 Folkways Records release, *Negro Folk Songs and Tunes*. Cotten went on to become a favorite at folk festivals in the late fifties and throughout the sixties.

ODETTA (1930–)

Odetta Holmes Felious, the most important black female folk artist of the folk revival period, was born in Birmingham, Alabama, on December 31, 1930. As a child, she showed an interest in music by playing notes on her grandmother's piano. When Odetta was six years old, she began to pursue her musical education. As a student in junior high school, she took voice lessons and became a member of the glee club. During high school she studied classical music, and after graduation she landed a role in a San Francisco production of *Finian's Rainbow*. That same year, at the age of nineteen, she was first exposed to folk music, and she began her career as a folksinger soon afterward. After achieving some popularity in the 1950s, she signed with Vanguard Records in 1960. Some of her recordings for this label, such as *Odetta Sings Folk Songs* and *Ballad for Americans*, featured traditional Appalachian folk music. Her style also incorporated African-American blues, jazz, and gospel music to create a versatile sound that continues to inspire folk artists today.

Young folkniks in Newport, Rhode Island, listen to a young man rehearse on the autoharp for his performance at the 1969 Newport Folk Festival.

In 1958 the Kingston Trio launched a new era in folk music with the release of their debut album *The Kingston Trio,* featuring the song "Tom Dooley," which sold more than three and a half million copies as a single. The group, consisting of Nick Reynolds, Bob Shane, and Dave Guard, offered listeners a homogenized, commercial version of folk music, with a repertoire that consisted largely of traditionally influenced, apolitical songs. With their close-cropped hair and trademark button-down shirts, the trio cultivated a wholesome image that made them appealing to older audiences as well as their peers. Their music reached such a wide market that *Life* magazine did a cover story on the group in 1959. Through their songs, a whole new generation was exposed to folk music, and the folk revival flourished. The Kingston Trio created a musical trend that continued into the early 1960s, giving rise to

THE KINGSTON TRIO

Formed in 1957, the original Kingston Trio consisted of Dave Guard (1934–1991), Nick Reynolds (1933–), and Bob Shane (1934–), three students who lived in northern California. Shane and Guard grew up together in Hawaii, and began playing and singing together in high school. Shane became friends with Reynolds while they were attending business college, and introduced him to Guard, who was a graduate student at Stanford University. The three shared an interest in folk, calypso, and Hawaiian music, and they started performing at parties and local clubs. Calling themselves the Kingston Trio, after the city in Jamaica, the group got their break when they filled in for comedienne Phyllis Diller at the Purple Onion, a small folk club in San Francisco where many folk artists were discovered. The trio played there for several months, and in 1958 they were signed by Capitol Records.

Their first album, *The Kingston Trio,* went to number one, with the help of songs like "Scotch and Soda" and "Tom Dooley." The latter became a tremendous hit when it was released as a single, turning the group into the first superstars of folk music. "Tom Dooley" was derived from an Appalachian ballad that told the story of Tom Dula, a convicted murderer who was hanged in 1868. Recorded in the 1920s by a blind fiddler from Tennessee named G.B. Grayson (1887–1930), the song was discovered in 1938 by Frank Warner (1903–), a folksinger and collector who heard it sung by Frank Proffitt (1913–1965) in North Carolina. Although the version recorded by the Kingston Trio was generally attributed to Proffitt, he never received any money from the song's sales.

The Kingston Trio spent most of the late fifties performing at clubs and college campuses all over the country. They also continued to record, releasing several albums before Dave Guard left the group in 1961. He was replaced by John Stewart (1939–), a twenty-one-year-old folksinger and songwriter who was a former member of the Cumberland Three. With this new lineup, the trio went on making records and touring until they disbanded in 1967, after producing more than thirty records in less than a decade.

During the fifties and sixties, coffeehouses were popular hangouts for young folk fans and beatniks in urban areas.

numerous other respectable collegiate-looking groups, including the Brothers Four, the Cumberland Three, the Chad Mitchell Trio, the Highwaymen, the Journeymen, and the Limeliters. While the Kingston Trio angered many folk purists with their popular influences and sanitized lyrics, they were probably responsible for inspiring some young people to discover more "authentic" folksingers such as Woody Guthrie.

One aspect of folk music that made it attractive to listeners was its participatory nature—in theory, anyone who could play a few guitar chords could become a folksinger. The Kingston Trio's popularity on college campuses everywhere made folk music a part of the lives of countless students, many of whom belonged to folk song clubs. As the 1960s began, numerous coffeehouses in urban areas such as Chicago, Cambridge, Berkeley, New York's Greenwich Village, and Toronto's Yorkville district also provided an outlet for new folk performers. Greenwich Village became the mecca of the folk scene, as it had been for the beatnik culture of the 1950s, prompting Alan Lomax to label those who came to join the Village's bohemian folk community "folkniks." A decade earlier, Charles Seeger had coined the term "citybilly" to refer to urban folksingers who attempted to identify with a rural way of life. The folk revival renewed interest in traditional folk music, encouraging the formation of groups like the New Lost City Ramblers, an old-time string band that included Pete Seeger's younger half-brother Mike, and the Greenbriar Boys, a trio of New Yorkers who played bluegrass material.

Many young, white, middle-class North Americans who had been brought up in the repressive culture of the 1950s saw folk music as a subtle means of rebellion against conformity. Most of the folk revivalists eschewed the clean-cut appearance of performers like the Kingston Trio, choosing a more natural look that usually included plain, simple clothing and longer hair. In a *Mademoiselle* article from the early sixties entitled "Folk Furor," Susan Montgomery noted that "Folk music, like a beard or sandals, has come to represent a slight loosening of the inhibitions, a tentative step in the direction of the open road, the knapsack, the hostel." The folk revival had become part of a larger cultural movement involving the youth of North America. Folk music was ready to serve as the soundtrack for the counterculture that would soon emerge—all it lacked was a charismatic performer to lead the way.

BOB DYLAN AND THE FOLK BOOM

The success of the Kingston Trio proved to the music industry that folk music was profitable, and record companies began to seek new artists who could continue the trend. When the first Newport Folk Festival was held in 1959, attracting an audience of thirteen thousand, a manager named Albert Grossman (1926–1986) remarked, "The American public is like Sleeping Beauty waiting to be kissed awake by the prince of folk music." That moment of awakening was not long in coming. In the fall of 1961, *New York Times* music critic Robert Shelton wrote a rave review of a performance by a twenty-year-old folksinger with "a cherubic look and a mop of tousled hair" that suggested "a cross between a choir boy and a beatnik." Bob Dylan had moved to New York at the end of 1960, driven in part by his desire to meet Woody Guthrie. He met Guthrie and Pete Seeger, and he frequented various spots in Greenwich Village, where he came to know Dave Van Ronk (1936–), Jack Elliott (1931–), and other local artists. Less than a year after he arrived in New York, Dylan signed a contract with Columbia Records, becoming one of the first young folksingers to be signed by a major label.

Released in early 1962, his debut effort, *Bob Dylan,* was not a huge commercial success—in the first year, only five thousand copies were sold. Dylan's first record consisted mainly of traditional folk and blues tunes, with only two of his own songs, "Talking New York" (a critique of the music

After moving to New York, Bob Dylan began to be recognized by the public as a folk performer who sang powerful protest songs in a distinctive voice.

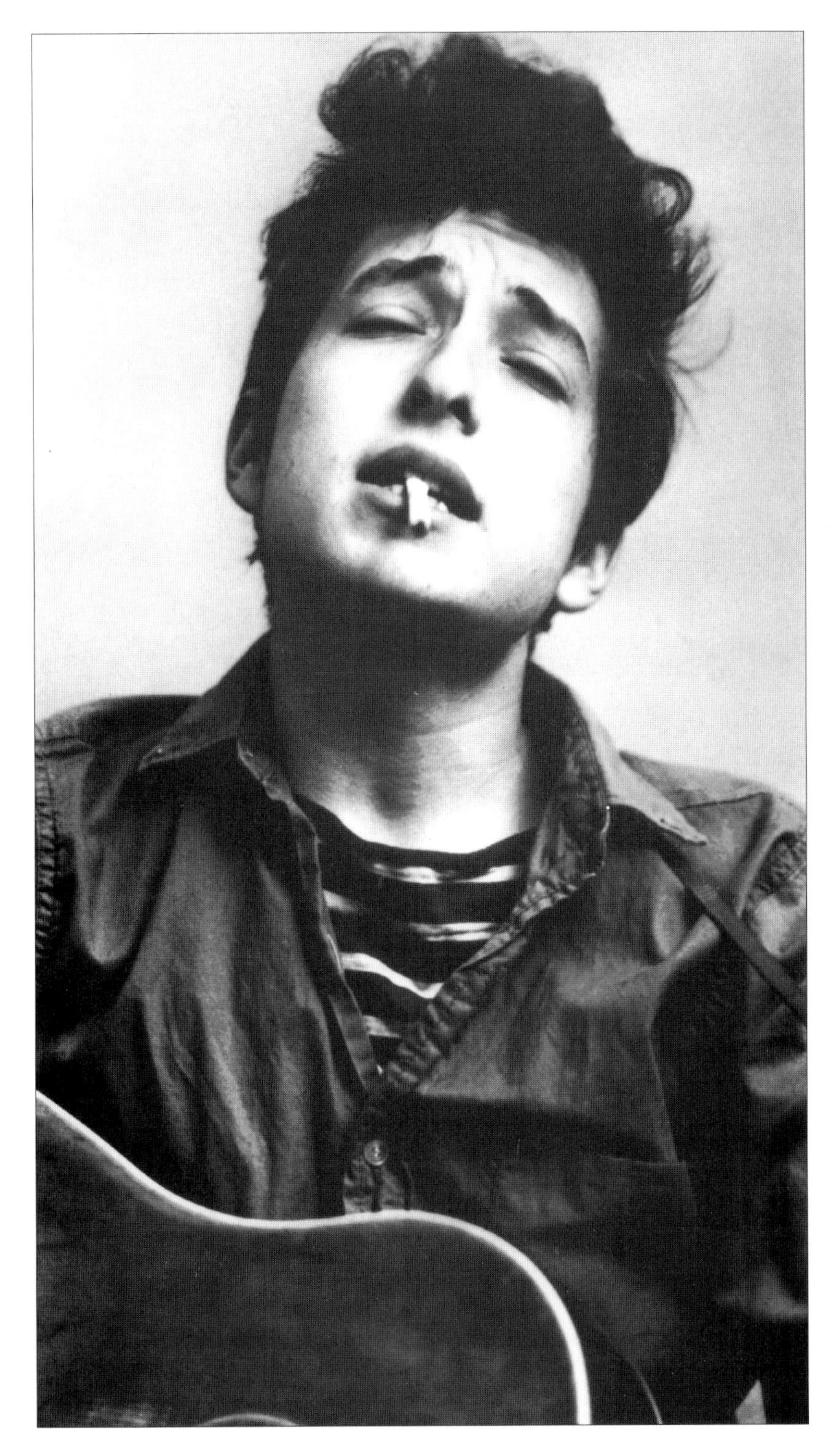

A young Bob Dylan adopts a Guthrie-like pose. Dylan's worship of Guthrie began when he was a student at the University of Minnesota.

A Cree Indian born in Canada, Buffy Sainte-Marie grew up in New England and became a folksinger and songwriter while attending the University of Massachusetts. She is known best for writing the song "Universal Soldier."

business) and "Song for Woody." By the time this album appeared in stores, however, Dylan had begun to concentrate more on his songwriting, turning out protest songs like "Blowin' in the Wind," which would soon be one of his best-known compositions. While songs of social commentary were obviously not a new creation, folk artists of the sixties like Dylan, Tom Paxton, and Phil Ochs revitalized the protest genre by focusing on contemporary issues such as the civil rights movement, the nuclear arms race, and the Vietnam War. Other songwriters like Buffy Sainte-Marie (1942–) and Peter LaFarge (1931–1964) drew attention to previously overlooked concerns, such as the oppression of Native American people. LaFarge's song "The Ballad of Ira Hayes," which became popular when country music star Johnny Cash recorded it in 1964, tells the story of a Pima Indian who helped raise the American flag at Iwo Jima during World War II. By the time the folk boom began to subside in the middle of the decade, folk music had become inextricably linked with social and political protest.

Most Americans remained unaware of Bob Dylan, although they did take notice of other new arrivals on the folk scene. In late 1962, *Time* magazine did a cover story on a young singer named Joan Baez, who had made a name for herself performing in Boston and at the Newport Folk Festival. With a repertoire consisting almost exclusively of traditional Anglo-American ballads, Baez had established herself as one of the musical purists

BOB DYLAN (1941–)

One of the most influential artists of the sixties, Bob Dylan has become a legendary figure in the history of American popular music. His career has spanned more than three decades, and his songs have been recorded by hundreds of artists.

When he first attracted attention in the Greenwich Village folk scene in 1961, he created a new identity for himself, telling people that he had spent his teenage years roaming the United States and playing with various blues and rock musicians. In fact, Dylan grew up in a middle-class Jewish family in Hibbing, Minnesota. Born Robert Allen Zimmerman, he taught himself how to play the piano, harmonica, and guitar by the time he reached his teens. Rock, blues, and country performers, particularly such stars as Hank Williams, Elvis Presley, and Little Richard made up his early influences. As a child he was fond of writing poems, and after he took up the guitar he began composing songs.

In the fall of 1959, Dylan entered the University of Minnesota, where he discovered the music of Woody Guthrie. Caught up in Guthrie's songs, Dylan read his autobiography and immediately adopted Woody as his new idol. He began performing at coffeehouses in the Minneapolis neighborhood known as Dinkytown, using the name Bob Dillon, which he later changed to Dylan. (According to one biographer, this name was probably inspired by the character Matt Dillon of the television show *Gunsmoke*, as well as a relative named Dillion.) After less than a year and a half of school, Dylan dropped out and went to New York, where he emerged as a gifted folksinger and songwriter who captured the nation's attention with his topical protest songs.

With the release of his fifth album, *Bringin' It All Back Home,* in 1965, Dylan abandoned overtly political themes and began writing lyrics that were more symbolic and introspective, and half of the record featured electric instruments. Although many folk fans were disappointed, Dylan found a new audience as a rock performer. His follow-up effort, *Highway 61 Revisited,* sold very well, with the help of his first big radio hit, "Like a Rolling Stone." As his career developed further, Dylan repeatedly proved to be an unpredictable artist. In the late sixties, he made a country record called *Nashville Skyline,* which included a performance by Johnny Cash. A decade later he produced *Slow Train Coming,* a collection of fundamentalist gospel songs that reflected upon his conversion to Christianity. Dylan's more recent efforts with the Traveling Wilburys, a band consisting of Dylan, George Harrison, Jeff Lynne, Tom Petty, and the late Roy Orbison, and his intermittent solo recordings suggest that he will continue to contribute to popular music for years to come.

PHIL OCHS (1940–1976)

Although Phil Ochs never achieved commercial success, he distinguished himself as a songwriter with ballads and protest songs such as "There But for Fortune" (1964), "Is There Anybody Here?" (1965), and "I Ain't Marchin' Anymore" (1965). Born in Texas, Philip David Ochs grew up in New York and Ohio. He attended a military boarding school and went on to study journalism at Ohio State University, where a friend introduced him to the music of Woody Guthrie and other folk artists. In 1961, after performing at Cleveland coffeehouses for several months, Ochs dropped out of school and moved to New York to become a folksinger. He quickly became part of the Greenwich Village folk scene, playing at clubs and spending time with Dylan and other artists. He performed at the 1963 Newport Folk Festival, where he received a standing ovation from the crowd. Ochs was signed by Elektra Records, and his first album, *All the News That's Fit to Sing,* was released in 1964.

Ochs was a political activist as well as a folksinger, and many of his songs focused on the issues of civil rights and the Vietnam War. He took part in numerous concerts to benefit antiwar organizations and various other causes. While his records failed to attract a large audience, Ochs was popular as a performer in such urban areas as New York and Los Angeles. Ochs' career as a recording artist ended in the early 1970s, and he slipped into obscurity. Despondent over his failure to achieve success as a topical songwriter, he committed suicide in 1976.

of the urban folk movement. Following the 1960 Newport Festival, at the age of nineteen, she turned down offers from major labels and signed a contract with Vanguard Records, an independent New York company. Her first album, *Joan Baez*, sold well, and a year later her second record, *Joan Baez 2*, became the first album produced by an independent label to be certified gold. Baez was also a popular concert performer, having made a successful tour of concert halls and colleges across the country in 1961.

Soon after being featured on the cover of *Time*, Baez gave Bob Dylan's career a major boost by inviting him to play at many of her concerts. She also helped to promote his material by singing his protest songs, including "With God on Our Side" and "Masters of War." Dylan's first important solo performance took place at New York's Town Hall in April 1963, and he was subsequently invited to appear on *The Ed Sullivan Show*. He declined after being told that he would not be allowed to perform his song "Talkin' John Birch Society Blues" (1963). This song was removed from his second album, *The Freewheelin' Bob Dylan,* shortly after it was released in May. The new record consisted almost entirely of Dylan compositions, and within a year it had sold more than 200,000 copies. That summer, Dylan was the star of the Newport Folk Festival, which drew a crowd of forty thousand people over one weekend. Dylan was now the undisputed leader of the folk movement.

In addition to performing together, Bob Dylan and Joan Baez were lovers during the mid-sixties. The dissolution of their romantic relationship was captured on film in D.A. Pennebaker's documentary *Don't Look Back.*

JOAN BAEZ (1941–)

Often referred to as the "Queen of Folk Music," Joan Baez exemplifies the connection between folksinging and politics. With her unyielding commitment to music and social issues. Baez was born on New York's Staten Island, on January 9, 1941. Her mother came from Scotland, and her father was a Mexican physicist. As a child, Joan lived in New York and southern California, also spending nine months in Turkey, Iraq, and Switzerland. Influenced by Odetta and Harry Belafonte, she sang in a choir and learned to play the guitar while in high school. Although she listened to a variety of music, her main interest was in traditional folk music, which she felt was more pure than rock and roll.

In 1958, the Baez family moved to Boston, where Joan studied drama at Boston University for a short time before becoming involved in the Boston-Cambridge folk scene. She performed at local coffeehouses, and made her professional debut in the middle of 1959 at the first Newport Folk Festival. After performing at Newport the following year, she released her first record, which set her on the road to stardom.

It was not long before she became known as a political activist as well as an entertainer. In addition to performing for charity benefits, taking part in antiwar rallies, and playing an active role in the civil rights movement, in 1964 she refused to pay a large portion of her taxes because the money was designated for defense spending. A year later she founded the Institute for the Study of Nonviolence in Carmel, California. During a demonstration against the draft and the Vietnam War, Baez was arrested for civil disobedience, and she served a short jail sentence. In 1968, she married David Harris, a former student leader who spent twenty months in prison for resisting the draft.

Baez maintained her career as a popular performer throughout the sixties, and her albums sold steadily. In 1972, after releasing almost two dozen records, on the Vanguard label, she moved to A&M Records where she created some of her most commercially successful songs, including "The Night They Drove Old Dixie Down" and "Diamonds and Rust." During the 1970s, Baez developed her skills as a songwriter and continued to tour and record. As the opening act at the Live Aid benefit concert in Philadelphia in 1985, she performed alongside much younger pop stars, evoking comparisons to the 1969 Woodstock Festival. The music of Joan Baez is still evolving today, and her recent release *Play Me Backwards* stands as evidence of her longevity as a folk artist.

In the middle of 1963, a popular folk trio known as Peter, Paul and Mary produced a single featuring two songs from *The Freewheelin' Bob Dylan*: "Blowin' in the Wind" and "Don't Think Twice, It's All Right." Their version of the Weavers' song "If I Had a Hammer" had been a hit the previous year, and their recording of "Blowin' in the Wind" went on to become the biggest-selling protest single ever made. Peter Yarrow, Noel Paul Stookey, and Mary Travers offered smooth, well-polished vocal harmonies and arrangements that appealed to a broad segment of the listening public. Of all the folksingers that came into prominence during the sixties, Peter, Paul and Mary were perhaps the most popular and undoubtedly the most commercially successful.

During this time, popular performers like Peter, Paul and Mary, along with other, lesser-known folk artists, maintained a commitment to social and political activism by becoming involved in the civil rights movement. In July 1963, Bob Dylan, Pete Seeger, and a few other folksingers went to Mississippi to play at a benefit concert for the Student Nonviolent Coordinating Committee (SNCC). That same month, the opening concert at the 1963 Newport Folk Festival ended with Seeger, Dylan, Baez, the Freedom Singers, and Peter, Paul and Mary joining hands for a powerful rendition of "We Shall Overcome." On August 28, 1963, more than a quarter-million people participated in the March on Washington, where they heard the famous "I Have a Dream" speech by Dr. Martin Luther King, Jr., and the musical performances of Baez (who led the crowd in "We Shall Overcome"), Dylan, Peter, Paul and Mary, Harry Belafonte, Mahalia Jackson, Odetta, and other artists.

With the release of his third record, *The Times They Are A-Changin'*, at the beginning of 1964, Bob Dylan established himself as a spokesman for the youth of America. The title song from his new album warned parents that change was imminent:

> Don't criticize what you can't understand.
> Your sons and your daughters are beyond your command.
> Your old road is rapidly aging.

Carl Oglesby, who once served as president of the radical New Left organization Students for a Democratic Society (SDS), noted that Dylan "gave character to the sensibilities of the Movement." A militant group that split from SDS in the late sixties actually named itself the

PETER, PAUL AND MARY

During a 1964 interview, one of the members of Peter, Paul and Mary commented, "Do you realize the power of Peter, Paul and Mary? We could mobilize the youth of America today in a way that nobody else could. We could conceivably travel with a presidential candidate, and maybe even sway an election." While this statement was certainly an exaggeration, as demonstrated by the group's involvement in Senator Eugene McCarthy's unsuccessful campaign for president four years later, Peter, Paul and Mary were immensely popular performers whose songs introduced countless Americans to folk music.

Noel (Paul) Stookey (1937–) was born in Baltimore, where he learned to play the guitar at the age of eleven. During the fifties, he organized a rock band for which he wrote some songs. While attending Michigan State University, he earned money performing as master of ceremonies in area clubs. In 1959 he moved to New York and began working for a company that manufactured photographic chemicals, but after discovering the Greenwich Village folk scene, he gave up the job to become an entertainer. Although he was interested in performing folk music, Stookey initially made himself known as a stand-up comedian. He met Mary Travers in 1961, and he persuaded her to begin singing with him.

Mary Travers (1936–) was born in Louisville, Kentucky, and brought up in New York's Greenwich Village, where she was exposed to folk music at an early age. As a child, she met Pete Seeger and other folk artists, and at fourteen she became a

member of the Songswappers, a group of young people that recorded three albums with Pete Seeger on the Folkways label. She sang occasionally at informal gatherings in the Village during her teens and early twenties, but never considered becoming a professional performer until she was approached by Peter Yarrow, who was interested in forming a folksinging group. (Mary, in turn, introduced Peter to Noel.)

Born in New York, Peter Yarrow (1938–) took violin lessons during his childhood and discovered folk music at the High School of Music and Art. Influenced by Woody Guthrie, Pete Seeger, and Burl Ives, Yarrow began performing folk songs while studying psychology at Cornell University. While at Cornell, he also helped a professor teach courses on folklore and folk music. After receiving his degree, he returned to New York, where his manager, Albert Grossman, came up with the idea of creating a folk trio. (Grossman later managed Peter, Paul and Mary, as well as Bob Dylan and other successful folk artists.) Yarrow, Travers, and Stookey began to rehearse, and Peter, Paul and Mary was born.

The trio took their name from a song called "I Was Born About 10,000 Years Ago," which contains the line, "I saw Peter, Paul, and Moses playing ring-around-the-roses," prompting Noel to change his name to Paul. In 1961, Peter, Paul and Mary played in coffeehouses across the country, and by the end of the year they were signed to Warner Brothers Records. Their debut effort, *Peter, Paul and Mary,* featuring the popular singles "If I Had a Hammer" and "Lemon Tree," went to number one in the middle of 1962. Their third album, *In the Wind,* was their most successful, and its version of Dylan's "Blowin' in the Wind" won them the 1963 Grammy Award for Best Folk Music Record. While many of their hits were songs composed by other folk artists, Peter and Paul wrote roughly half of the material performed by the trio. In addition to being enormously popular performers, Peter, Paul and Mary were among the first well-known folk artists to promote civil rights issues and to oppose the Vietnam War.

The group broke up in 1970, shortly before the song "Leaving on a Jet Plane" (written by pop star John Denver) became their last hit. During their nine years together, eight of the ten albums they recorded went gold and five went platinum. Each member of the group went on to pursue a career in music to some degree during the 1970s, but none of them achieved any significant commercial success. After reuniting for a tour in 1978, the trio realized that they still had an audience for their songs from the sixties. Since then, Peter, Paul and Mary have performed together intermittently, continuing to popularize their form of folk music.

"WE SHALL OVERCOME"

More than 200,000 people participated in the historic March on Washington, which was intended to raise public awareness and to make the central government sit up and take notice of the civil rights movement.

The history of the song that became an anthem for the civil rights movement in the 1960s offers an excellent example of the ways in which folk songs may be altered over time to suit different purposes. In 1901, the Reverend Charles Albert Tindley (1851–1933) composed a gospel hymn entitled "I'll Overcome Someday." This song, which was also known as "I'll Be All Right," was spread across the South through African-American churches. Many years later, in 1945, when the black men and women of the Food and Tobacco Workers' Association in Charleston, South Carolina, went on strike, they sang a new version of the song on the picket lines, changing the title and the lyrics to "We Will Overcome." This adaptation of the song was discovered by Zilphia Horton, who taught at the Highlander Folk School, located near Knoxville in the mountains of eastern Tennessee. She wrote additional verses and introduced the song to others at the school.

Highlander had been founded by Horton's husband, Myles, a former theology student, in 1932. Until the 1950s, when the school began to hold interracial workshops designed to fight racism, it served as a labor college, where rural workers learned how to organize unions. Guy Carawan (1927–), a folksinger and song collector who was the school's musical director, rewrote "We Will Overcome" as "We Shall Overcome" in the late fifties to create an inspirational song to be used in the civil rights movement. Southern civil rights workers who learned the song at Highlander began to sing it as they took part in sit-ins and protests, and by the early sixties it was firmly established as the movement's theme song.

Weathermen, after a line in Dylan's song "Subterranean Homesick Blues." Yet as Dylan's lyrics became a voice for the emergent counterculture, Dylan himself withdrew from politics and the protest scene. He became less concerned with projecting a social consciousness, and his music soon came to reflect this change.

At the 1965 Newport Folk Festival, Dylan shocked and angered many in the audience by coming on stage with an electric guitar to play "Maggie's Farm" and "Like a Rolling Stone." Pete Seeger reportedly cried as Dylan

THE FREEDOM SINGERS

The original Freedom Singers (left to right): Charles Neblett, Bernice Johnson (Reagon), Cordell Hull Reagon, and Rutha Harris.

The Freedom Singers consisted of four African-American students and civil rights activists who in 1962 formed an a capella quartet to support the civil rights movement then organizing in the South. Modeled after traditional community-based gospel and jubilee quartets and on the Almanac Singers, the original Freedom Singers were Rutha Harris (1940–), Bernice Johnson (1943–), Charles Neblett (1941–) and Cordell Hull Reagon (1943–), all field secretaries for the Student Nonviolent Coordinating Committee (SNCC). This ensemble successfully toured communities across the United States for a year, performing concerts of freedom songs in churches, concert halls, and schools as a way of informing, organizing, and building support for the civil rights movement.

The first Freedom Singers disbanded in late 1963, although there have been sporadic reunions since 1980, and a second group, this one an all-male version (also SNCC field secretaries), began performing in early 1964. This group included Rafel Bentham, Emory Harris (Rutha Harris' brother), James Peacock, the brothers Matthew and Marshall Jones, original member Charles Neblett, and guitarist Bill Perlman. The second Freedom Singers performed live concerts, recorded, and helped to raise funds for SNCC until they disbanded in 1966.

Bernice Johnson Reagon (married for a short time to Cordell Hull Reagon) went on to a career as an unaccompanied solo folk performer and recording artist. During the late sixties, she began organizing cultural festivals and tours featuring traditional and contemporary singers. In 1973 she founded Sweet Honey in the Rock, an a cappella ensemble of African-American women. Reagon continues to perform and record with this group and is also well known as a scholar in the field of African-American cultural traditions.

performed, and a large portion of the audience responded by booing and hissing. Dylan returned later that night with an acoustic guitar to perform "It's All Over Now, Baby Blue" and "Mr. Tambourine Man," but the damage had already been done. Folk music's favorite son had been seduced by rock and roll, and his songwriting had become less topical and more introspective. While other folk artists would continue to carry on the folk tradition, the heyday of folk music, and the folk song revival, had come to an end.

FOLK-ROCK

The end of the folk boom that had begun in the 1950s was marked by the introduction of new sounds in popular music. A musical movement that became known as the British Invasion began when the Beatles came to America in 1964 with a new sound that revitalized rock and roll. That same year, an English band called the Animals released an electric version of "The House of the Rising Sun," a song that had been discovered by Alan Lomax in Kentucky in 1937 and recorded by various folk artists, including Bob Dylan. The song went to number one, and the concept of mixing folk with rock became an established trend when a California group known as the Byrds had their first hit single with "Mr. Tambourine Man," a Dylan composition, early in 1965.

With their music, the Byrds opened the door for numerous other folk-rock artists, including Donovan, the Lovin' Spoonful, the Turtles, and the Mamas and the Papas. In the fall of 1965, a former member of the New Christy Minstrels named Barry McGuire (1937–) recorded "Eve of Destruction," a folk-rock protest song that went to the top of the charts, selling over a million copies. The following year brought Simon and Garfunkel's hit "The Sound of Silence," an electric version of a song they had originally released in 1964 on *Wednesday Morning, Three a.m.*, an acoustic folk album that failed to sell. Fifteen-year-old Janis Ian (1951–) established herself as a singer-songwriter in 1967

Folk-rocker Janis Ian is known best for her 1967 hit "Society's Child," which she wrote when she was only fifteen years old.

THE BYRDS

Originally consisting of Roger McGuinn (1942–), David Crosby (1941–), Gene Clark (1941–1991), Chris Hillman (1942–), and Michael Clarke (1944–1993), the Byrds were largely responsible for creating the style of music that became known as folk-rock. McGuinn, the leader of the group, came from a folk background, having played with the Limeliters and the Chad Mitchell Trio. While living in Greenwich Village, he recorded with Judy Collins before moving to Los Angeles, where he encountered Clark, a former member of the New Christy Minstrels, and Crosby, who later became part of Crosby, Stills and Nash. McGuinn wanted to create a new kind of music that combined aspects of folk and rock. As he put it, "If you took Lennon and Dylan and mixed them together...that was something that hadn't been done before." He was one of the first rock musicians to play a twelve-string electric guitar, which helped give the Byrds their distinctive sound.

The group's first two albums, *Mr. Tambourine Man* and *Turn! Turn! Turn!*, featured several songs written by Bob Dylan ("All I Really Want to Do" and "The Times They Are A-Changin'") and Pete Seeger ("The Bells of Rhymney" and "Turn! Turn! Turn!") as well as original material. In 1966, the Byrds became pioneers in the psychedelic rock genre with the release of a single called "Eight Miles High," from their third album. Although the Byrds continued to record, undergoing a number of changes in personnel, the group's popularity faded in the late sixties, and they dissolved in 1973.

with "Society's Child," a folk-pop song that addressed the problems of an interracial high school romance. A number of other performers who blended elements of folk and country with rock and popular music, including Buffalo Springfield, Joni Mitchell (1943–), the Band, Linda Ronstadt (1944–), Country Joe and the Fish, and Crosby, Stills and Nash, also became well known during the mid- to late sixties.

THE LEGACY OF FOLK

While folk music no longer captures the attention of consumers as it did in the 1960s, it continues to have an impact on popular music in a variety of ways. The success of contemporary pop artists whose songs exhibit a folk influence, such as Tracy Chapman, the Indigo Girls, R.E.M., Suzanne Vega, Michelle Shocked, and The Cowboy Junkies, is one example of the continuing legacy

The spirit of Woody Guthrie lives on in British songwriter Billy Bragg, whose music serves as a reminder that performers can educate as well as entertain.

Many of Suzanne Vega's songs offer thought-provoking social commentary. "Luka," which is perhaps her best-known composition, addresses the issue of child abuse.

of folk music. Singer-songwriters such as Nanci Griffith, Mary Chapin Carpenter, and Emmylou Harris all draw from folk backgrounds to create music that appeals to fans of folk and country music. And in light of the recent popularity of so-called unplugged recordings by rock musicians, acoustic music is making at least a temporary comeback. Although most mainstream performers tend to shy away from making political statements with their music, lesser-known artists such as Billy Bragg, a British devotee of Woody Guthrie whose albums feature such songs as "There Is Power in a Union," promote the leftist politics so often connected with folk material. Despite a current scarcity of traditional-style folksingers, the folk artists of North America have created a legacy that will endure for many years to come.

BIBLIOGRAPHY

Baez, Joan. *And a Voice to Sing With: A Memoir.* New York: Plume, 1987.

Baggelaar, Kristin, and Donald Milton. *Folk Music: More Than a Song.* New York: Crowell, 1976.

Brand, Oscar. *The Ballad Mongers: Rise of the Modern Folk Song.* New York: Funk & Wagnalls, 1962.

Dunaway, David King. *How Can I Keep From Singing.* New York: McGraw-Hill, 1981.

Hood, Phil, ed. *Artists of American Folk Music.* New York: William Morrow, 1986.

Klein, Joe. *Woody Guthrie: A Life.* New York: Knopf, 1980.

Lomax, John A. *Adventures of a Ballad Hunter.* New York: Macmillan, 1947.

Lornell, Kip. *Introducing American Folk Music.* Madison, Wis.: Brown & Benchmark, 1993.

Rodnitzky, Jerome L. *Minstrels of the Dawn: The Folk-Protest Singer as a Cultural Hero.* Chicago: Nelson-Hall, 1976.

Seeger, Pete. *The Incompleat Folksinger.* New York: Simon & Schuster, 1972.

Shelton, Robert. *No Direction Home: The Life and Music of Bob Dylan.* New York: Beech Tree Books, 1986.

Stambler, Irwin, and Grelun Landon. *Encyclopedia of Folk, Country and Western Music.* New York: St. Martin's, 1969.

SUGGESTED READING

Denisoff, Serge. *Great Day Coming: Folk Music and the American Left.* Urbana, Ill.: University of Illinois Press, 1971.

———. *Sing a Song of Social Significance.* Bowling Green, Ohio: Bowling Green State University Popular Press, 1983.

DeTurk, David A., and A. Poulin, Jr. *The American Folk Scene: Dimensions of the Folk Song Revival.* New York: Dell, 1967.

Hampton, Wayne. *Guerrilla Minstrels.* Knoxville, Tenn.: University of Tennessee Press, 1986.

Lieberman, Robbie. *My Song Is My Weapon: People's Songs, American Communism, and the Politics of Culture, 1930–50.* Urbana, Ill.: University of Illinois Press, 1989.

Rosenberg, Neil V., ed. *Transforming Tradition: Folk Music Revivals Examined.* Urbana, Ill.: University of Illinois Press, 1993.

Willens, Doris. *Lonesome Traveler: The Life of Lee Hays.* Lincoln, Nebr.: University of Nebraska Press, 1993.

Woliver, Robbie. *Bringing It All Back Home: Twenty-Five Years of American Music at Folk City.* New York: Pantheon, 1986.

SUGGESTED LISTENING

Baez, Joan. *The First Ten Years.* Vanguard.

Byrds, The. *The Original Singles.* Columbia.

Dylan, Bob. *The Times They Are A-Changin'.* Columbia.

Guthrie, Woody. *Dust Bowl Ballads.* Rounder.

——· *Library of Congress Recordings: Three Hours of Songs and Conversation Recorded by Alan Lomax.* Rounder.

Kingston Trio, The. *Capitol Collector's Series.* Capitol.

Ochs, Phil. *There and Now: Live in Vancouver, 1968.* Rhino.

Odetta. *Odetta at Town Hall.* Vanguard.

Peter, Paul and Mary. *Ten Years Together—The Best of Peter, Paul and Mary.* Warner Brothers.

Seeger, Pete. *We Shall Overcome: The Complete Carnegie Hall Concert.* Columbia.

Various artists. *Don't Mourn—Organize! Songs of Labor Songwriter Joe Hill.* Folkways.

Various artists. *Folk Classics: Roots of American Folk Music.* Columbia.

Various artists. *Folk Song America: A Twentieth-Century Revival, Volumes I–IV.* Smithsonian.

Various artists. *Folkways: A Vision Shared—A Tribute to Woody Guthrie and Leadbelly.* Columbia.

Various artists. *Songs of Protest.* Rhino.

Various artists. *Troubadours of the Folk Era, Volumes I–III.* Rhino.

Weavers, The. *Greatest Hits.* Vanguard.

INDEX

PHOTOGRAPHY CREDITS

©Joe Alper: p. 63

AP/Wide World Photos: pp. 15, 48

Archive Photos: pp. 44, 62

Archive Photos/Frank Driggs Collection: pp. 9, 55

The Bettmann Archive: pp. 6–7, 8, 21, 40 top, 40 bottom

©Larry Busacca/Retna Pictures Ltd.: p. 67

©John Cameola/Globe Photos: p. 56

©Theodore Donaldson/FPG International: p. 45

Frank Driggs Collection: pp. 17, 18, 19, 24, 49

©Ray Flerlage/Michael Ochs Archives: pp. 46, 58

FPG International: pp. 20, 22–23

Globe Photos: p. 32

©Patricia L. Hollander/FPG International: p. 30

©Andrew Kent/Retna Ltd.: p. 64

©Pearl Korn/Globe Photos: p. 27

Courtesy of the Library of Congress: p. 16

©Betty Nettis/FPG International: p. 50

Michael Ochs Archives: pp. 10–11, 12, 29, 52, 53

Photofest: pp. 25, 60–61

Popsie Randolph/©Frank Driggs Collection: p. 41

©David Redfern/Retna Ltd.: p. 36

©Richard Robinson/Globe Photos: p. 47

©Paul Slattery/Retna Pictures Ltd.: p. 66

©Gene Trindl/Globe Photos: p. 65

UPI/Bettmann: pp. 14, 34, 35, 38–39, 40 middle (2), 42, 43, 54, 57